# Niagara Falls

## By Sarah De Capua

**Consultant**
Linda Cornwell
National Literacy Specialist

Children's Press®
A Division of Scholastic Inc.
New York   Toronto   London   Auckland   Sydney
Mexico City   New Delhi   Hong Kong
Danbury, Connecticut

Designer: Herman Adler Design
Photo Researcher: Caroline Anderson
The photo on the cover shows part of Niagara Falls.

**Library of Congress Cataloging-in-Publication Data**

De Capua, Sarah.
    Niagara Falls/ by Sarah De Capua.
        p. cm. — (Rookie read-about geography)
    Summary: A brief introduction to Niagara Falls and some things
to do there.
    ISBN 0-516-22016-0 (lib. bdg.)        0-516-27392-2 (pbk.)
    1. Niagara Falls (N.Y. and Ont.) Juvenile literature.
[1. Niagara Falls (N.Y. and Ont.)]  I. Title. II. Series.
F127. N8D33      2001
917.13'39—dc21                                        99-42013
                                                      CIP

JE
DEC
c. 1

$14.25

# Do you know what makes a waterfall?

4

When water from a stream
or river falls from a high
place to a lower place,
it is called a waterfall.

Niagara Falls is a famous
group of waterfalls located
between New York State
and Ontario, Canada.

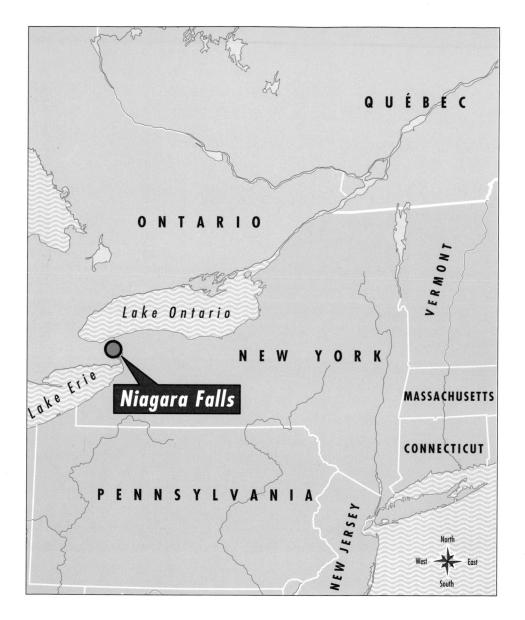

QUÉBEC

ONTARIO

Lake Ontario

VERMONT

NEW YORK

MASSACHUSETTS

CONNECTICUT

Lake Erie

*Niagara Falls*

PENNSYLVANIA

NEW JERSEY

North

West ✦ East

South

Niagara Falls is on
the Niagara River.

The Niagara River makes
up part of the border
between the United States
and Canada.

Niagara Falls has three waterfalls. The American Falls and Bridal Veil Falls are in the United States. They are separated by a small piece of land called Luna Island.

American Falls     Luna Island     Bridal Veil Falls

Bridal Veil Falls          Goat Island          Canadian Falls

The Canadian Falls is in Canada. Goat Island separates the Canadian Falls from Bridal Veil Falls.

The Canadian Falls is also called Horseshoe Falls. It gets this name because it is U-shaped, like a horseshoe.

15

Every year, millions of people visit Niagara Falls. It is one of the world's most popular vacation spots.

Many visitors enjoy riding boats called *The Maid of the Mist*. These boats go very close to the water at the bottom of the falls.

People on the boats wear
raincoats so their clothes
do not get wet!

Visitors can also climb towers to get a better view of the falls.

The roaring water is very noisy!

Some people walk through a tunnel behind Horseshoe Falls. It is fun to see the inside of a waterfall.

Others visit the Cave of
the Winds on Luna Island.

There they can see
American Falls and
Bridal Veil Falls up close.

Throughout the year, colored lights shine on Niagara Falls at night.

Every Friday during the summer, fireworks are set off over the falls.

There are other interesting
places to visit nearby,
including museums,
monuments, and parks.

# Most people want to see Niagara Falls first!

# Words You Know

American Falls and Bridal Veil Falls

fireworks

Goat Island

Horseshoe Falls

*The Maid of the Mist*

waterfall

31

# Index

# About the Author

Sarah De Capua is an author and editor of children's books. She resides in Colorado.

# Photo Credits

Photographs © 2002: AP/Wide World Photos/Bill Sikes: 29; Corbis-Bettmann: 16, 27, 30 bottom (Richard T. Nowitz), 21 (Hubert Stadler); Liaison Agency, Inc./Getty Images/Mark Lewis: 4, 31 bottom right; Photo Researchers, NY: cover (Martin Bond/SPL), 26 (Brian Yarvin); Superstock, Inc.: 6, 8, 11, 12, 15, 18, 22, 28, 30 top, 31 top left, 31 top right, 31 bottom left; Woodfin Camp & Associates: 3 (Dilip Mehta), 19, 25 (Mike Yamashita).

Map by Bob Italiano

AAY-6312